The Circular Spiral (and the contingent ascension)

A short collection of convoluted, dusk words with a luminous yet coarse finish.

*Best served cold with a dash of melancholy and a glass half full of optimism (or rum).
By D9C

I'm a drug addict; have been for over a decade, and I haven't even reached my dirty thirties yet. Those first four words may make up a portion of my personality but I've never once let them define me.

Long before the greenery, pills, chemicals, opiates, cloudy smoke, unknown substances and dosages that defy my mortality, there were words, and my enigmatic relationship with them since I could first pen crayon to paper. My mother claims that as a toddler I ran up to her at night and proclaimed that I had taught myself to read, although my earliest memories of writing stem from kindergarten where we were asked to keep a diary and add one sentence a day. I managed to finish the diary in a matter of days, stopping at one sentence wasn't enough for me, I was enthralled the second my pencil touched the page. Since then I've always kept some form of diary or journal, yet reflecting over the last decade of entries has proven to be insightful, terrifying and progressive simultaneously.

I have always managed to find literary salvation in the darkest of times, hence my love for contrast and writing in its rawest, most stripped back form. From scrawling down jilted, cryptic passages after being awake for a hundred hours to spending hours lost scribbling down poems in a sober, clear and crescent state of reverie.

My ongoing recovery has proven to be both a mammoth, poignant set of stairs and a clarity filled jar of epiphanies. I no longer care for the substances that I once couldn't picture living life if they were void. Yet I have now come to embrace that empty void and the realization it brings with it; the realization that life on its own, original and unadulterated dose is a beautiful concept. Discovering joy again in simple scenarios that were once shrouded and jaded in a thick layer of self-deception but are now transparent has felt akin to seeing the ocean for the first time.

As you will see my passages contain both sides of my bilateral coin; from the highest of my drooping lows to my eventual, metrical self-discovery and desire to inspire.

I hope that you find something beneficial buried somewhere within my writings. I'll let my words speak for themselves.

d9c

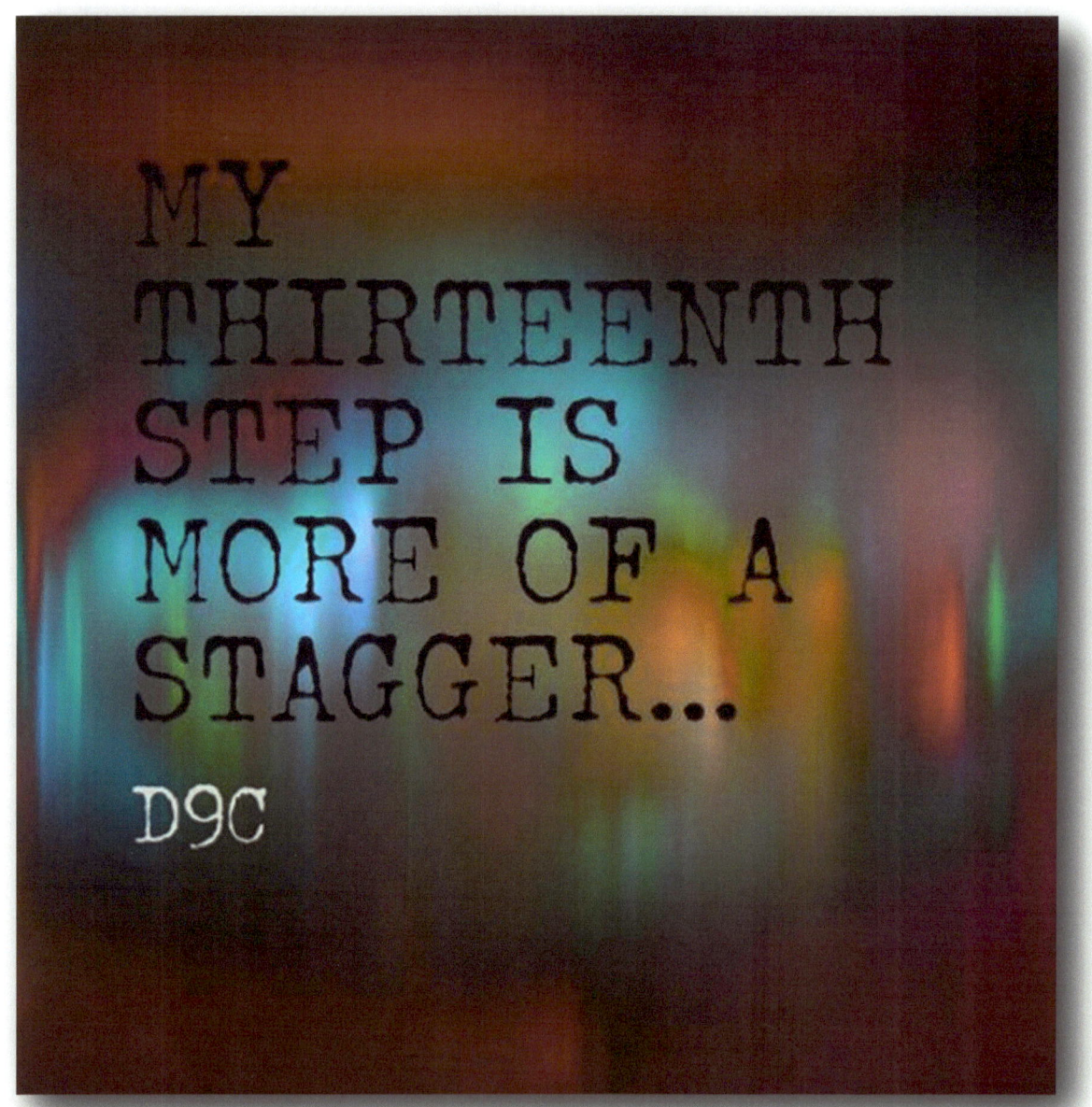

4 The Circular Spiral   Alex Di Carlo

The blind strafing into the blind

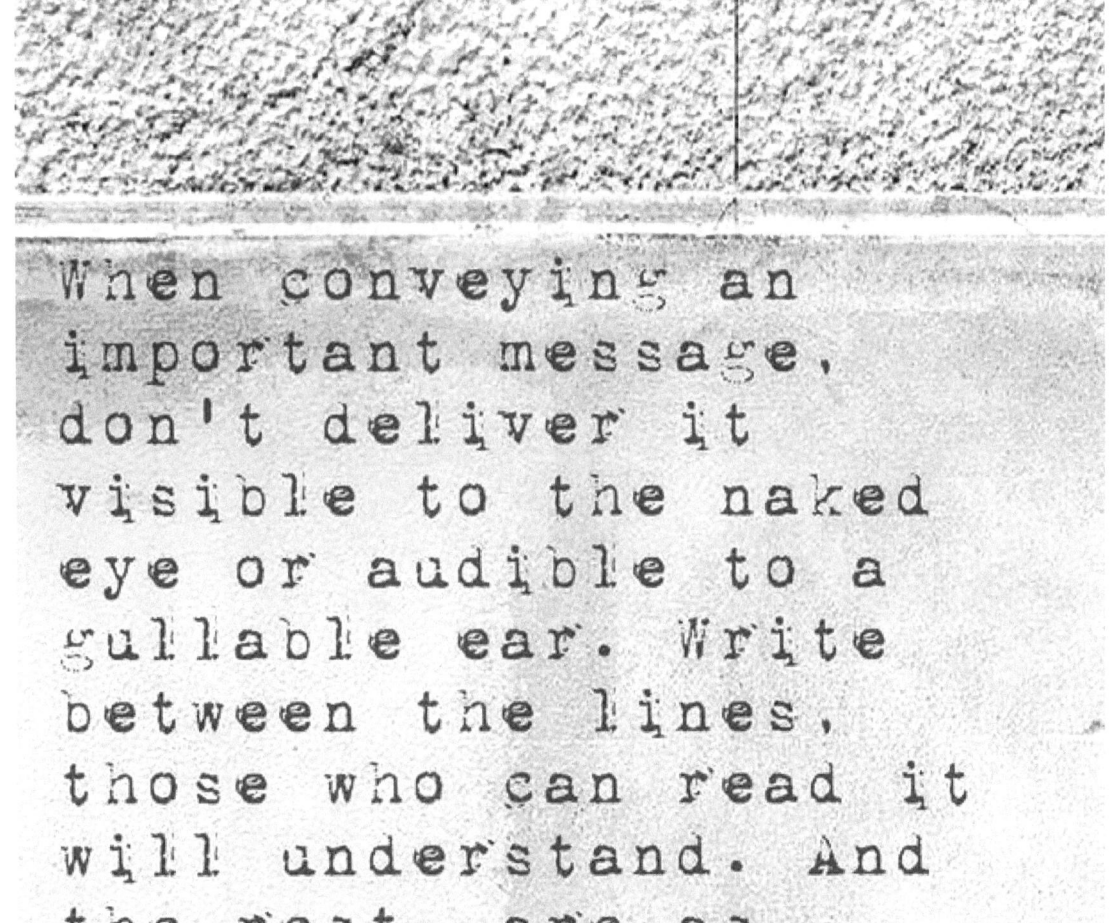

When conveying an important message, don't deliver it visible to the naked eye or audible to a gullable ear. Write between the lines, those who can read it will understand. And the rest, are as useful as three day old butchers off cuts.

The start of the spiral...

"I'm a user, not an addict." He proclaimed, full of opiate derivative driven vigor. As he wiped his frail hand across his black, deteriorated sleeve for the third time in as many minutes it dawned on Dante that the person he once knew was now void in the shadows. Dante just had to put the broken mirror down and stop repeating the second sign of madness. Sometimes self reflection can be the cruelest of wake up calls.

Self-critique until I'm obsolete

What's with the year long cold you caught in spring?

Why is the house littered with empty pharmacy bags?

When you said you were sick last week, what did you mean?

What's with all the apathy?

You know these questions are rhetorical right...? You're a mess.

(and the contingent ascension)

> "I'll only do drugs on days that end in 'Y'."

The J journals:
He started to notice his scattered Sundays trickling down into Mondays and Wednesdays. With each mid-week slip he swore it to be a finale. The last chapter of a book with the edges so frayed and the paper so faded it read like a begotten burden.

DgC

V.O.I.C.E.S

He remains ignorantly blissful of the covert and hollowing whispers playing over ever so softly inside of his fragile head. They come by the droves, riding horses as high as their prolific, recognition driven personalities will allow them to. Hell bent on the reformation and decentralisation of his scarred neurons. Their subliminal, rodent like voices are indistinguishable amongst one another as they pry in and attempt to subdue irrational thought. As the years trickle by and the vile pharmaceuticals begin to take their toll he is left alone. Alone in the truest sense of both the word and the world. Might he one day vanquish these voices, might he one day feel free again.

(and the contingent ascension)

10 The Circular Spiral   Alex Di Carlo

Aviation deviation

She talks into the nothingness as her eyes turn to fixate their bleak gaze towards my confused retina. I could barely make out what she was saying, her words jumbled like a fallen jenga board game. "I don't trust bird watchers." She mumbled both angrily and anxiously. "There's something strange about a person who is so transfixed on flying. What are they trying to fly away from?". And then it hit me. A mind is a precious thing to lose.

(and the contingent ascension)

J Journal entry - Equality

He often told himself that self criticism is the best form of self improvement, but in the process was oblivious to the internal bleeding that emitted from his sub conscious.

He saw raw potential in numerous people around him, yet a thousand mirrors reflecting his talent couldn't boost his self esteem.

He knew of his shortcomings, his perils and the chemical thorns in his side that plagued him like a locust, and just when he thought he had weeded them out, they would grow back thicker than ever.

"There has to be more than this." he pondered with equal parts hope and fear.

To be continued...

Lead by example- Astray

The J journals:

How can something so somber be so beautiful in a truthful contrast?

This escapism is forcefully bleached black, void of all colour yet brimming with a hedonistic glow of opportunity.

That's what it all boils down to right? The here and now. No matter how elusive you try to be, you're with us still in the present; and we're forever grateful.

Early onset/ memorabilia

I'm always forgetting to remember or remembering to forget; for better or worse.

Untitled

Human Tourniquet

I'll try and stop the bleeding. If I could take your pain away and make it mine, I would.

(and the contingent ascension)

Uncle Chop

ALWAYS BITE THE HAND THAT FEEDS. YOU NEVER KNOW IF THAT MOTHERFUCKER IS GOING TO POISON YOU. JUST BECAUSE YOU'RE BEING PARANOID, DOESN'T MEAN THERE AREN'T CUNTS OUT TO GET YA.

Information sensation

Snort your snapchats
Inject your tweets
Smoke your notifications
Swallow your messages

You're now mainlining the most widespread, easily accessible, lobotomy mimicking drug. You're more wired than a tweaker on a 72 hour bender writing down licence plates as the cars drive past.

I read online that internet addiction has risen by 210% in three years. But the following article claimed that 34% of all statistics are made up.

As the thin, binary line between communication, entertainment and information begins to distort our senses, we are left in withdrawal. Sure, better than lying painfully in a fetal position sick from opiates; but the scary part is, we're just getting started.

Untitled #2

Euphemism in greyscale.

The horse you rode in on had its decrepit hooves bound ankle deep in a pool of your tears.

Its height was merely a shadow reflected from a stained brick wall of emotions rendered with your insecurities.

Fuck cats

You were just like a cat, everything was on your prerogative. You only wanted attention when it was on your terms. Loyalty wasn't on your agenda.

Well, lucky I'm a dog person.

Fuck love

Depression from lost love is temporary. No matter how deep the cut is and how agonizing the pain may be.

Eliminate co-dependency from your state of mind and replace it with self reliance. Love to live, don't long and live for love to come around and save you from yourself.

(and the contingent ascension)

Fucking

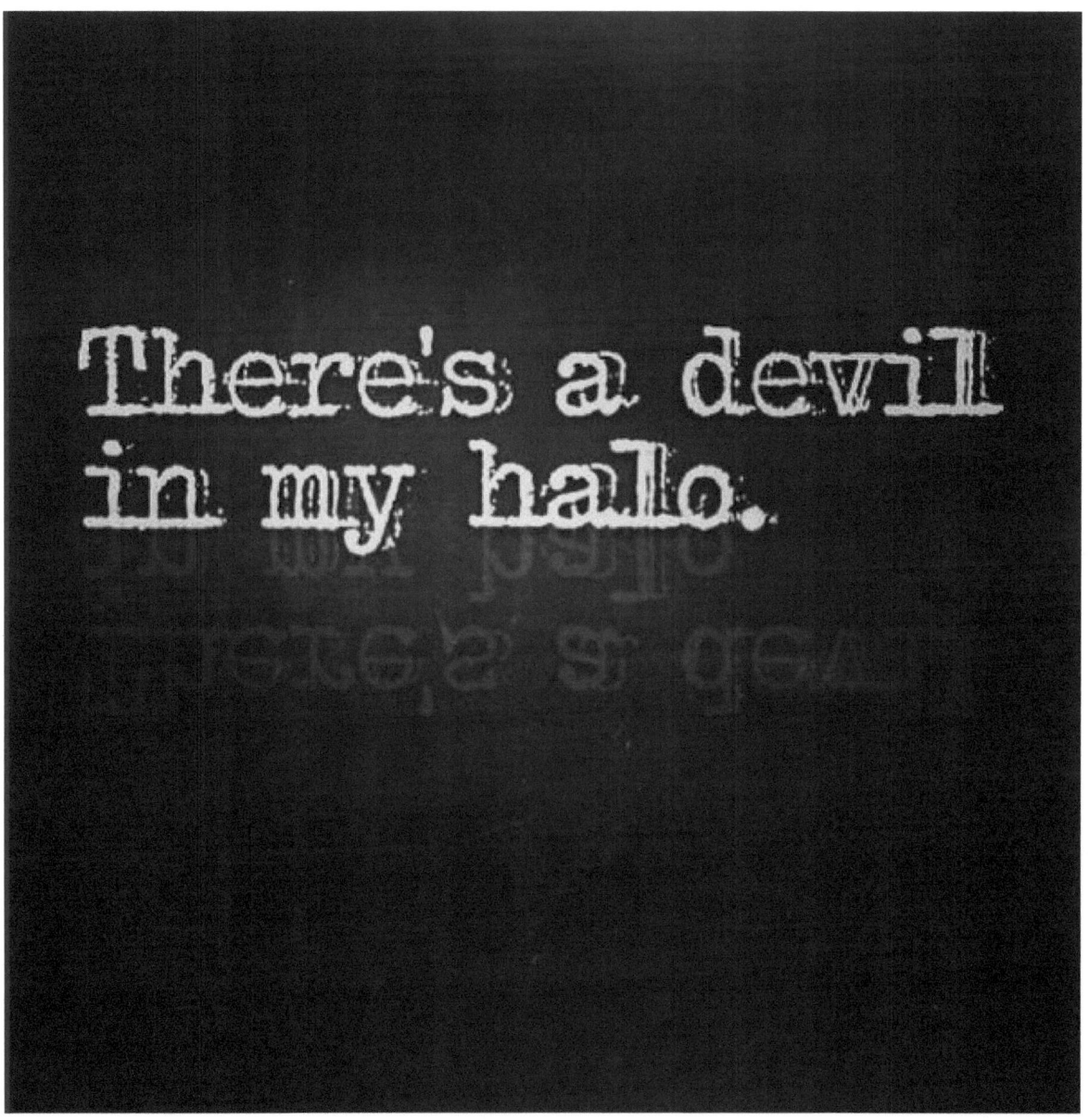

(and the contingent ascension)

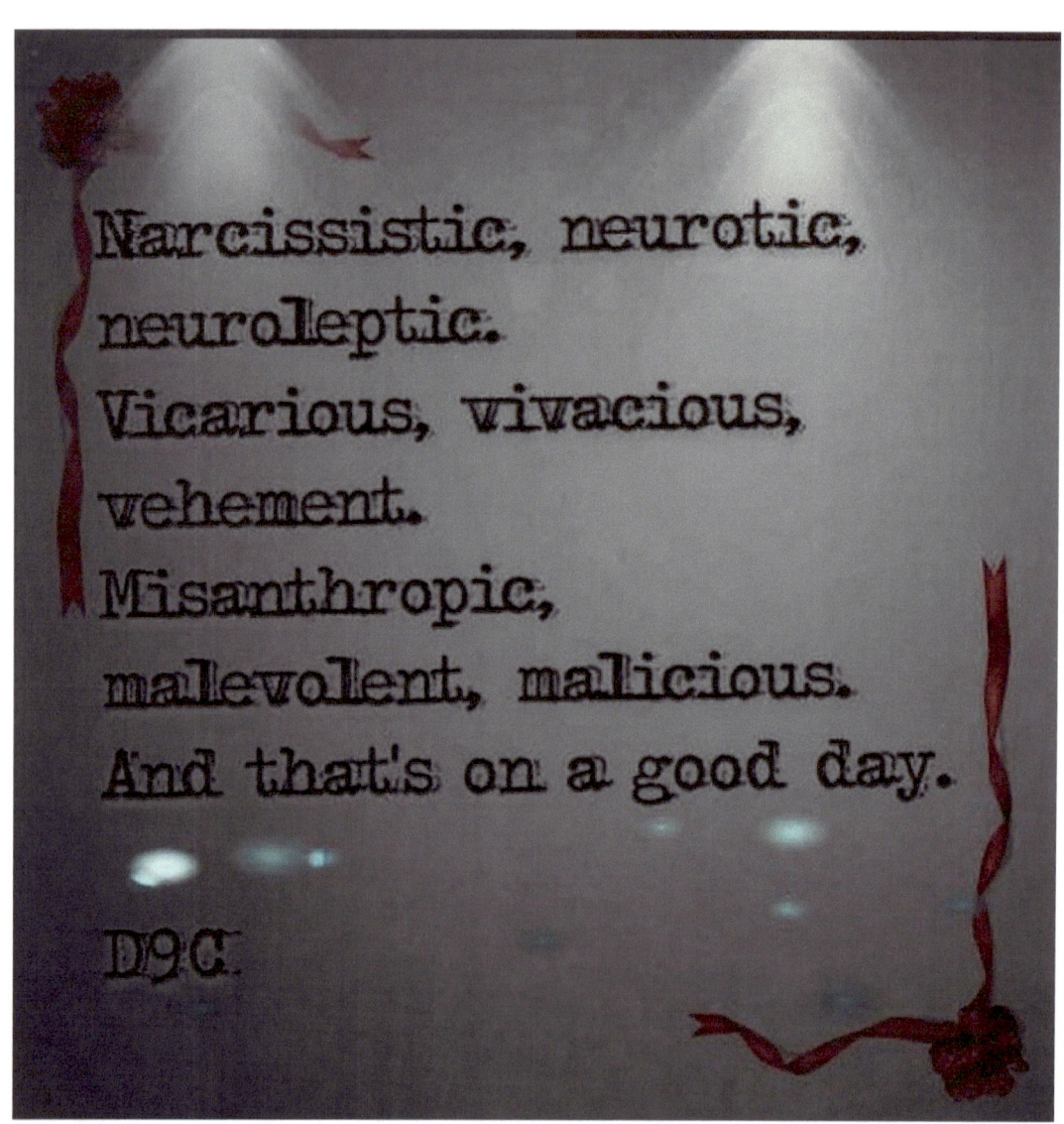

The Circular Spiral — Alex Di Carlo

"You're a hedonistic nihilist. A misanthropic humanist. A vengeful saint. A pessimistic optomist. You're a walking, talking breathing contradiction and a Fucking paradox. But I still love you, you crazy Fuck."

And with that, Dante smiled a wry, lukewarm smirk into the shaded mirror and went back to bed.

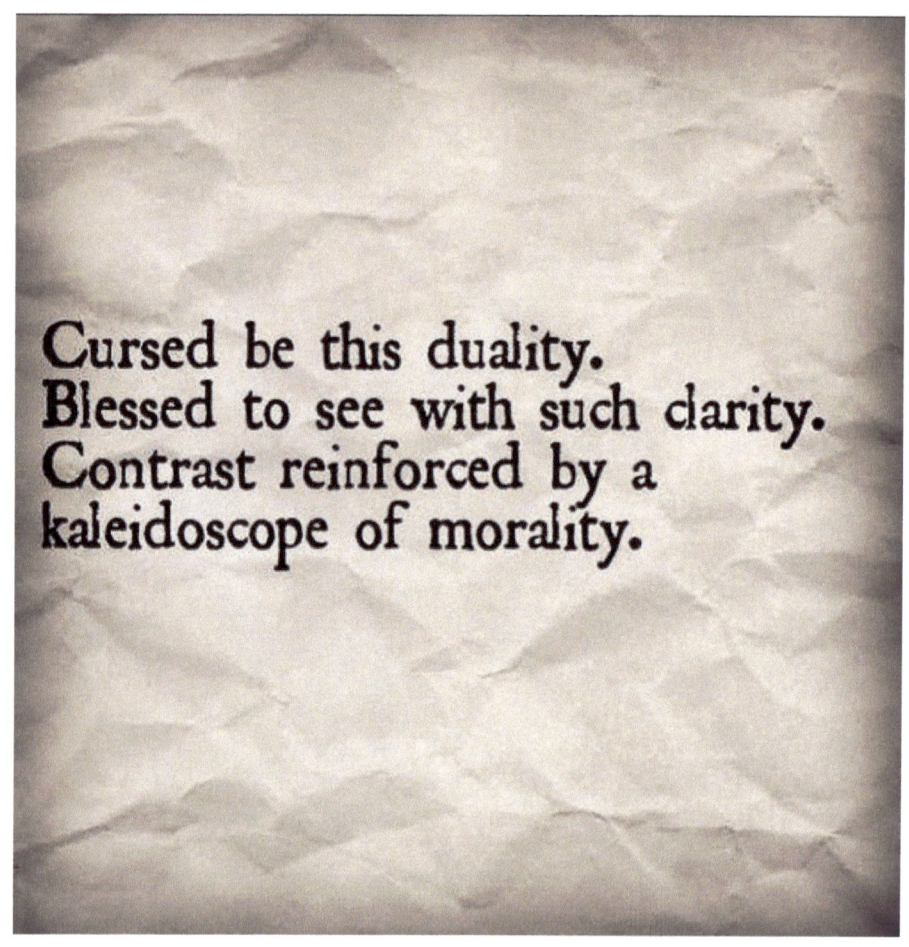

The Circular Spiral

Alex Di Carlo

I SAW YOU OUT OF THE CORNER OF MY JILTED PERIPHERAL. YOUR MERE PRESENCE STAINED A VIVID IMPRESSION INTO THE SOFT FABRIC OF MY REALITY. BUT I WOULD SOONER BURN OUT MY EYES THAN BARE THE BURDON OF WITNESSING SUCH A BEAUTIFUL CALAMITY ANEW.

-D9C-

(and the contingent ascension)   D9C

Always know when you're on tilt, and if you realise that you are; adjust your day to the rythm of the slant.

D9C

We can't see your scars. No matter how visible you believe them to be.

And then suddenly; akin to a change of the weather, I just stopped giving a fuck about what 'they' thought, saw or heard.

Ever since that landmark day, I've had the truest, most sincere sensation of what it means to be me.

(and the contingent ascension)

"You're just not consistent." She said flatly, whilst my darting eyes glanced around the room but finally found thier home in her transfixed, forward gaze.

"It's not that I intentionally have a desire to be inconsistent and I understand that it may be frustrating as my mind jumps from one endeavour to another adventure. But being enslaved to a state of normalcy for me is a fate worse than death."

"I follow the sun, and if you aren't on board to join me in my quest to enrich and broaden our dim horizons then it's best for both of us that we take the positives from the good times spent and part ways."

And with that, she turned an ignorant cold shoulder and walked away. Hopefully the next fellow she finds will have a relationship checklist similar to the ending of trainspotting.
-D9C-

Just another flower memorial on the roadside highway.

"You wouldn't do it, would you Dante?" She said hesitantly, illustrating a dark picture of his personal outlook on euthanasia.

He shuffled his feet anxiously to the left, took a deep breath and with tears in the corner of his eyes he responded in a soft, croaky voice:

"In a perfect world, the idea of visiting an early purgatory and escaping this pain feels as if it's my only option. But I digress; I was put here for a purpose higher than my own selfish, carnal desires. I breathe to heal. I can transcend my own vapid existence into a beacon of help for those around me. I don't want to be revered; I just want to be."

The rising sun sees
whichever colour of
chameleon you desire to
ink into your deception
for the day.

Yet you are a singular
and constant shade of
truth beneath the
shadows of the moon.
d9c

You are so much
more than the
worst thing
you've ever
done.

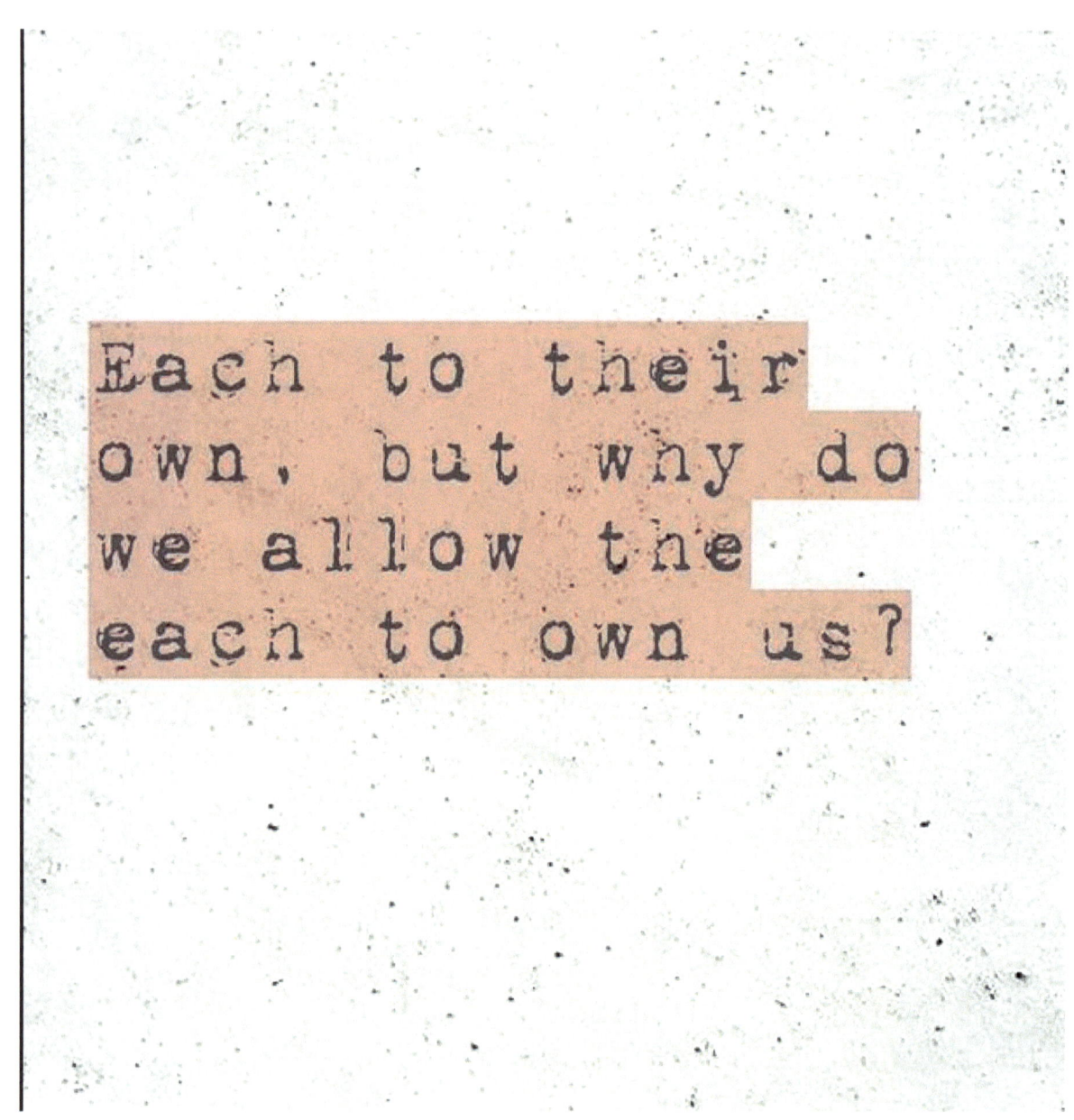

(and the contingent ascension) D9C 37

A shallow figment of a dusty, diluted imagination is all that I remember of you.

Before the toxic chemicals gradually infused their way into your developing neurones. Before you witnessed first hand, the vicious violence that human beings are capable of. Before the lucidity. Before realising, yet endlessly repeating the definition of insanity...

There existed only you; and nothing in the known world could penetrate your convictions, your perplexing and intricate disposition; or the unexplainable sensation you felt whilst you were left to your own rose coloured devices.

Bittersweet it may be; even if it shall remain just a mere, fragmented figment; the embers from the fire it ignited will continue to burn until they're extinguished and the flailing ashes echo your words, imbedded in a timeless capsule of a post millennial paperback.
D9c

Sullenly encroached amongst the rising tide of questionable decisions made in the scorching temperature of the here and now, he gazes back blankly at the immense energy yearning to be unshackled and begotten of chemical burden.

Condensed within his seemingly ordinary yet vastly transparent reflection, his eyes sing forth hymns laden with past trauma and present acceptance. He finds the two nouns far from mutually exclusive; with the latter forming and reinforcing a core conviction that laid concealed. And with that at the forefront into his journey of progression, his lips slowly part to form a wry smile. As the silent songs continue to sing, it dawns on him that although he can't take back the past; the latter noun will forever mend it.

(and the contingent ascension)

Ode to my chemical friends and enemies.

We were once bound inward by the purest strain of diluted blood. We shared vast memories of tragedies passed and reconciled time after time over moments now left in exile. You were mine and I was yours- although looking back without the rose colored lense I lean more towards the latter. Even though we held the same hand, you always seemed to emerge the victor.

Yet it is now, with a light heart and a clear mind that I bid you farewell. A bleak good riddance left in a purgatory of our old and decrepit self despair. Goodbye old friends.

Substitution is an application best left as a negative deviation from the jilted proclamation that sobriety is a one way affirmation.

Far be it from the truth that recovery isn't merely twelve golden steps to an illuminated enlightenment and a shiny, tingly feeling of fulfillment; rather he has found it to be a visceral ball of condensed emotions. Unleashed unconditionally in every which way, internally repairing battered neurons and externally mending broken relationships.

Delving deeper into the minds eye he sees it fitting that the crooked, neon entry sign above the dimly lit door reads "WORK IN PROGRESS".

(and the contingent ascension)

Letter to your current self,
03/08/2006

Well, It's been a long road hasn't it?
You cheated an early grave twice, spent unforgiven time between four walls and countless hours wide awake when you should've had your frayed head resting on a pillow. You've buried friends with welted eyes, lost many more to the chemical abyss and realised the hard way who will be there when the proverbial shit spins around the fan like a cyclone.

Evidently though, like you always used to say "you can't have light without darkness." Now I'm no seer, but I have an obtuse feeling that although your shadow will always linger; that contrasting light is due to shine down in the near future. Change is growth, and growth is progression. Peace.
D9c

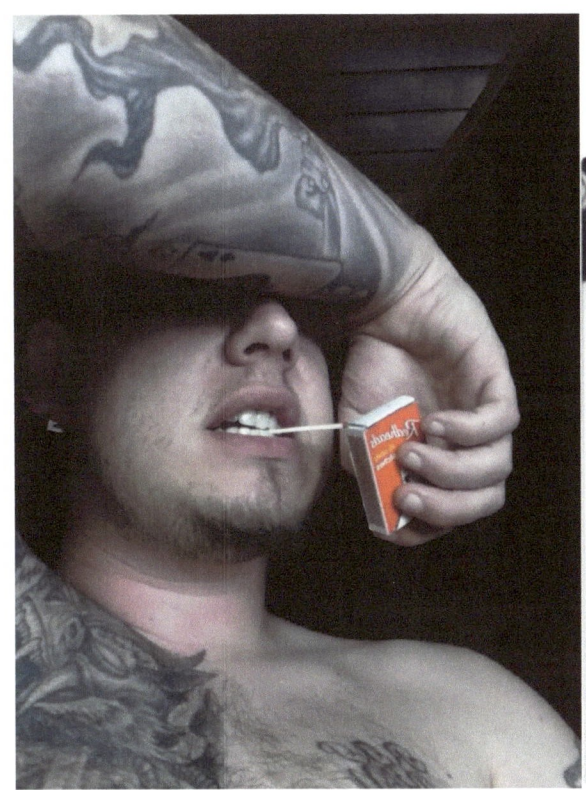

www.ingramcontent.com/pod-product-compliance
Lightning Source LLC
Chambersburg PA
CBHW042010150426
43195CB00002B/84